THE 10 SECOND SALE

Write Emails That Help You Sell Smarter, Sell Better, and Sell More

David Traub

David Traub
David@SellBrilliantly.com

To Dawn, my wonderful wife. You are the best friend, wife and partner I could have ever hoped for. Thank you for your patience and support while I've worked on this endeavor.

To my boys, thank you for teaching me the patience necessary to accomplish a project of this nature. You both have a determination and work ethic that makes me proud.

Thank you to my customers and many mentors over the years, for teaching me these lessons that I now can share with others.

Table of Contents

Introduction

10 Seconds. That's all the time you have to get your email replied to, if they are even gong to bother. Your prospect needs to be able to decide they are going to read your email, read it, consider it and hit reply within 10 seconds.

I've spent my entire career in sales. I'm a front line salesman; It's all I've ever done, and it's all I can imagine doing. In 1986, as a recent high school graduate, and a flaming introvert, I was clueless about what I wanted to do with my life, all I knew for sure was that I did not want to go into sales.

Since that time, I've been in the top 5%-10% of multiple sales teams, personally produced 10s of millions of dollars' worth of sales, helped those I've managed or coached generate over $100 million in sales, personally ran over 7,000 face- to- face sales meetings and made well over a quarter of a 1/4 million sales phone calls.

I'm often asked what my favorite sales books, courses, and tools and resources are. Without a doubt, my favorite sales resource is the humble email. I'm not talking about using an auto-responder or sending mass emails;. I'm talking about targeted emails to one lead, prospect or customer at a time.

Once you understand the the theory behind great sales emails and how to use the included templates, you'll be able to customize and send them out quickly and start getting many more 10 second sales.

Let's look an example of how email can dramatically improve your sales numbers: Assuming that you close 25% of your opportunities and you have to reach out to 20 leads to generate an opportunity. That means for every one1 sale, you have to reach out to 80 leads. Of those 80 leads which you reach out to, four become opportunities. Those are not bad numbers when you look at it that way. On the other hand, that also means that 95% of your leads did not turn into opportunities and less than 2% became sales.

If typically you close just one sale a week on average; What if you could convert just one more lead, (out of 80) into an opportunity each week?. With only a 1.25% improvement in converting your leads into opportunities, you would be generating an extra 13 sales each year (a 25% increase). Effective use of sales emails can easily do that for you. Just a slight improvement in your ability using to use email to convert your leads into prospects will dramatically increase your sales productivity.

It's important to note that **Sales emails** and **Marketing emails** have different purposes, and as such get constructed differently if you want great results. For example, if you want to make sunny side up eggs, you wouldn't put the eggs in a bowl and beat them first. You'll learn in this guide how to follow the right recipe for great sales emails.

These are not long- or medium- form sales letters designed to get a person excited to purchase your product, or to take them to a sales page where you'll finish the pitch, reveal the price and offer them a guarantee or the like. Much of what you learn here will be different than what you have read about email marketing. Since you want a different result, you need to follow a different recipe. In a marketing piece you generally try to get people to acknowledge that you are out there, that you exist, what you do, and what your message, and then drive them to an opt-in or sales page.

These emails are designed to get a response. Either to get your foot in the door for a one- on- one conversation with your prospect, or to move a sales forward through the sales process.

There can be a lot riding on your emails – managing them so effectively has been an integral factor in my ongoing success. I've spent years of frustration and headaches putting in the legwork to try and find ways of securing the next sale; email has consistently helped me to do that. It helps me get to the right person at the right time, allowing prospects to call attention to themselves and let me know when I should be reprioritizing them up or down on my target list.

In a sales email you're objective is to get a reply. Usually the reply you want is agreement to a call or meeting. Sometimes I'll be to be a referral, or get a testimonial. You don't want them to get distracted by your copy, or website, a detail on your sales page, so you'll need to craft the emails to quickly generate enough interest, curiosity and value that they will hit the reply button. The more they have to think after seeing your email before deciding to reply, the less likely you will get what you want.

In this book, you will learn some of the secrets of exactly how top-producing sales reps (those who generate over $1,000,000 in sales revenue annually) use email to dramatically impact their results. You'll learn how to craft a great email, how to leverage your time sending emails and the best tools to use with your emails, as well as also getting access to 43 of my favorite revenue-producing email templates. These come complete with a breakdown on how to modify each and every single one for your own individual use AND downloadable, editable versions of each, so that you can get started right away.

These emails and what you'll learn here are the result of years upon years of work and have literally resulted in over $10 million in sales and hundreds of thousands of dollars in commissions to me personally.

Within this book you'll learn to:
- Set up calls and meetings with your target customers and other busy people
- Get what you need from a select number of contacts
- Follow up while impressing your prospects
- Connect easily with the influential
- Boost your email productivity dramatically, and
- Stand apart from your competition and just about everyone else

*****WARNING**: Do not just skip over the lessons revealed here and just swipe the email copy. MUCH better results will follow if you understand the lessons first.

All the best,

David

Sales emails 101

Why email is important

Since its inception in 1971, email has grown to be a huge part of our daily lives. In fact, it's grown so much that in 2012, it was estimated by Radicati.com that 144.8 BILLION emails were sent worldwide, each day.

On average, people spend around 11.2 hours reading and answering emails each week. That's 28% of a 40-hour work week; and with mobile usage growing quickly, more people are spending even more time on their email and less on the phones at their desks, making them harder than ever to reach by phone.

Even though research has found that only one in four emails is essential for work, and only 14% of work emails are considered critically important, your prospect is likely spending much of their time there, you need to be able to reach them there. Furthermore, taking into account how quickly people scan their emails for what is important, you need to be able to make yours stand out, be easy to digest, easy to respond to and, most importantly, easily demonstrate your value to your prospect.

While nothing beats a face-to-face conversation with your prospect, that is also the most expensive and time-consuming method. With high-dollar sales or long sales cycles, a one-on-one meeting (in person, or online) will usually be required, but there are great ways at ensuring these meetings have the potential to be fruitful before committing. Email allows you to communicate quickly with a prospect and start a conversation before you ever get them on the phone or meet with them. It's a great way to leverage your time, and with a good library of standard emails which can quickly and easily be customized for each recipient, you can potentially reach more prospects than you can with any other method.

However, I should make it clear that I don't recommend this as your sole method of communication; in fact, just the opposite. My favorite use of emails is simply to make sure that I get a chance to connect with customers and prospects by phone or face-to-face. Properly used, email can result in many more appointments scheduled each day than previously was possible.

Why most sales emails fail

As important as email is to your sales cycle, the truth is that most sales emails fail. There are a number of things which cause these failures:

1. **Failure to make sense**. Before you send an email, it's important to ensure that you have grammatically put the words in your email together in a coherent manner. All too often, sales reps send emails which barely make sense. If you don't take the time to clearly and professionally articulate your thoughts, you'll simply make your prospect want to NOT deal with you.

2. **Failure to include a call to action**. Next, it's important to understand that simply being able to grammatically put words together in a way which makes sense is very different to writing an email that will get a response. If your email does not make it clear that you'd like a response AND make it an easy response to give, it's unlikely that you will get one. Unfortunately, many sales emails have no call to action at all.

EMAIL COMMANDMENTS: There are several critical concepts contained in this book, which I like to call "Email Commandments". I'll draw attention to them throughout the book and there is a complete list in Appendix A.

EMAIL COMMANDMENTS #1 AND #2:
1) Include a Call to Action, and
2) Make it easy to Reply

---

3. **Failure to follow your own instructions**. Even worse, an email often ends with telling the prospect that you'll call them by a certain date... and then you don't. This may sound obvious, but I've seen a number of email selling systems which propose

sending emails with no call to action and simply telling the prospect that you will call them Tuesday (or whenever), yet lots of people using those emails do not adequately track who they are to call when and as a result fail to make the proposed call. This completely destroys any credibility you might have before you ever have your fist contact with the prospect.

4. **Failure to get opened**. If your email is never opened, you will never get a response. Having a great subject line is critical to this. Often, your subject line is the only thing people will read. Later on in the book we'll discuss subject lines in more detail.

5. **Failure to send to the right medium**. You need to make sure that you are sending your message to somewhere where it is appropriate. Sending a message on Facebook is usually a bad idea: it doesn't allow for organizing emails or forwarding them to others, and is often just simply not where your target

wants to get work messages. Spend the time to properly research your prospect and send your email to their email address.

6. **Failure to get to the point**. People are trying to get through their emails quickly; they often even only read them on their phones. Especially when you don't have a relationship yet with the person you are sending to, it's critical that you do not make your emails too long, too wordy or without a clear and obvious purpose. Otherwise, you'll simply get skipped over or, even worse, deleted.

7. **Failure keep the email brief**. Don't put too much info in your email. You should not have your whole pitch or your entire list of potential benefits in the email. Brevity is key to getting a reply. Remember you are not selling your solution in the email, you are simply trying to generate personal contact between you and the prospect.

8. **Failure to be easy to read**. Formatting counts. If you don't use multiple paragraphs and spaces

between paragraphs (and/or indents), your message will be hard to read. If your paragraphs are too long, they are hard to read, especially on a mobile device. If it's hard to read, and you're prospect isn't already itching to meet with you, then you won't get read. Don't get read, and you won't get a response; and your next email may be ignored before they even read the subject line. Make liberal use of spacing, short sentences and bullet points to make your message easy to consume.

EMAIL COMMANDMENT # 3:

Make the format of your email easy to read

---

9. **Failure to remember third-grade English**. Yes, spelling counts. Punctuation counts. Make sure your message meets proper standards, or you'll look unprofessional and your message won't matter to your prospect. Along similar lines, don't use texting abbreviations in a sales email.

10. **Failure to read your own email**. All too often we

think what we have written makes sense and looks good, without checking it. Don't assume that just because you knew what you meant, your intended message is what made it on the page. Moreover, don't assume that just because you knew what you meant, anyone else will. Read your work OUT LOUD to yourself before sending. That will clear up many simple mistakes. This is especially true if you have auto-correct, as often what it supplies will not be close to what you meant. To see what I mean, take a look at http://www.sb1.us/ikov .

Understanding the busy mind

To ensure the best chance of getting your emails opened, responded to and resulting in a real conversation taking, you've got to understand the mind of a busy person. Most likely you target people who are not just sitting around, sipping a cappuccino staring at their inbox while hoping and praying that you might write to them. Instead, it's likely your targets are professionals with a lot going on.

If that's the case, you need to realize that the average decision-maker in a business:

- Receives more than 100 business emails a day (if they have more than four employees working for them, double that number).
- Has 10 or more newsletters which they have subscribed to arrive each day.
- Receives more than 25 personal emails every day.
- Receives more than 50 emails every day from salespeople like you.

This doesn't even include the whole slew of emails they get advertising Canadian pharmacies, Viagra and other completely nonsensical spam.

These people usually have multiple projects which they are working on and which demand their attention. Indeed, there are a lot of people who demand their attention and as a result, they are brutally protective of their time. If you looked at their laptop, you'd not be able to read "Delete" on the keyboard of many, due to the key being so worn from overuse. At the same time, these people likely rose to their position by being professional. If you can establish credibility, uniqueness and value, they will want to connect with you.

This makes it essential that you send emails targeted to the right person, that are different from the others they get and that allow them to quickly digest the core of the message while seeing value in it in a glance. You don't have a minute; you don't have 30 seconds, or even 15 seconds. If you do not have an established relationship with the person you are emailing and you are not a known entity to them, you have merely a glance (that's it!) to make an impression.

Persuasive Sales Emails

You're going to need to put time and effort into persuasive emailing. It's a skill, like any other, that takes time and practice. The good news is that much of what you will need to email will be repeated. Once you've got it down, you can use it over and over again. The templates which follow will help; however, you should still spend some time really working on your own email voice.

"More than a half, maybe as much as two-thirds of my life as a writer is rewriting." — John Irving

I'd love it if every time I sat in front of my keyboard to send an email, the perfect words just flowed out of me. Instead, much of what comes out of my fingers fits precisely what Anne Lamott refers to in her instructional book on writing, Bird by Bird, as "shitty first drafts".

When you have just a glance to capture your audience, it's more than critical to be effective with your writing. Once you've written your first draft, go back and read it out loud. Then rewrite it. After you've gotten something you really like, copy the snippets to a folder, an Evernote document, a Word document or somewhere that you can find and use them again.

However, I realize that just saying, "Go back and rewrite it," is not unlike reading a recipe for the ultimate yummy, gooey, chocolate cake and finding the final instruction is simply: "Put it in the oven and cook until done." You need to know what temperature, for how long and how to tell when it is done. To that end, here are some suggestions on where to start.

1. So What? Make every sentence pass the "So what?" test. Consciously or sub-consciously, every reader is going to ask themselves this as they read your email. Don't wait until they ask. Ask it of yourself before you click "Send". If there isn't a clear answer, either rewrite it or scratch it completely.

EMAIL COMMANDMENT #4:

Make Every Sentence Pass the "So What?" Test.

---

2. No Passive Voice. Remember eighth grade English. Mr. Monroe, my eighth grade teacher, had a rule about the passive voice: Don't use it. Every assignment I turned in came back marked accordingly (usually with an excessive amount of red ink!). Based on my performance in that class, he'd probably not believe that I listened, but I still remember that lesson. While a place for the passive voice exists (in scientific or technical writing), you'll have much more compelling copy if you avoid it completely in sales emails.

Don't remember your own eighth grade English? Verbs are either active (when you attend the Compelling Offers Webinar, you will learn six ways to structure your offers so that clients feel compelled to accept, now) or passive (The Compelling Offers Webinar will be one of the most productive uses of your time). Ultimately the purpose of your sales efforts is to drive audience to take action… and to take it now! Active verbs make your words have more drive towards movement and make your pitch feel much more alive. In a short email, you need to maximize the impact of every word. Active verbs help accomplish this.

Strengthen your verb usage with this quick exercise: After you write your email (or any sales copy), go through it to identify every time that you have used any form of the verb "to be," and look for ways to replace it or punch it up a bit. You don't need to eliminate EVERY instance of passive voice in longer copy, but in your short sales copy you should. Often you can find the right verb to punch the copy up directly after the form of "to be" that you used. At the same time, look for unnecessary words to eliminate.

For example, let's look at the sentence: "Our Making Magic Offers webinar is revolutionary in generating sales, and one of the things it does is it amplifies your customers' need, so that they take action now."

In that sentence, the phrase "one of the things" does nothing to enhance the message – so it can go. Using "amplify" as the main verb would change this to: "Our Making Magic Offers webinar is revolutionary in generating sales. It amplifies your customers' need, so that they take action now."

Once you've made your first pass through, go back through one more time and look for more ways to eliminate unnecessary words. After another pass, this same phrase can become: "Our Making Magic Offers webinar revolutionizes sales generation, amplifying your customers' need so they take action now."

The resulting phrase strengthens your message,

calling attention to the action.

If identifying passive voice isn't a strength of yours, a free online tool called the Hemingway Editor does a great job of identifying problems in your writing, including passive voice, for free. Just go to www.hemingwayapp.com and paste your text into the editor.

3. Remove Jargon, Cliches and Generalities. Just because you understand jargon, that does not mean your audience does. When you send an email to your prospect and they don't understand it, don't expect a reply. While you understand the difference between a direct response offer and brand marketing, assume they don't. Write your sales emails without using those terms.

Clichés – by definition – are over used. Standing out from your competition gives you dramatically better results, so don't use verbiage which everyone else does. Along the same lines, generalities don't do you any good. Everyone says they are "the best XXXX on the market." Don't let yourself sound like everyone else; instead give them a specific selling point and tell them why you are the best. Instead, try saying something like "We are the only Mobile Website Developer which GUARANTEES you'll at least double the number of leads you get."

4. Keep it short. You'll hear this a lot. In your sales emails, short is important. These emails are not meant to be long-form sales copy. Go through your writing and look for long sentences, then replace them with shorter ones. The easier they are to read, the more likely you'll get the reply you want. Shorten phrases. Eliminate words. Anything you can do to make your message clearer is worth the effort.

EMAIL COMMANDMENT # 5:

Keep Your Email short

---

5. Get a second opinion. While you can't do this before you send every email, have others look at the templates you plan on using. Just because something made sense to you, does not mean it will make sense to someone else.

Follow up

I can't say enough about how important great follow-up is to your sales efforts. It's critical to every step of your sales process to build follow-up into your routine. That applies to your sales emails, too.

With the marketplace as cluttered with sales and marketing messages as it is today, I've heard that it can take five or six attempts to contact a prospect before they are even consciously aware that you are trying to communicate with them. That means that the first four or five times that you call, email or put your ad in front of a prospect, it won't even register. You need to repeat the process if you want success.

Despite that, over 70% of unanswered emails end the entire email chain after one email! Make sure that isn't you. When you send that killer sales email to a new prospect and they don't respond, don't end the process there. Call them. You'll likely get their voicemail; that's fine. Leave a message. What should you say? Essentially, say the same thing you said in your short intro email. I've got a great guide on how to craft a call opening which doubles as a great voicemail message. You can get a free copy by following the simple instructions at the end of this section.

Still no reply? Send another email. I have several cold and warm prospecting emails that I use. Each will highlight a different benefit, success story or example. Using the templates provided in this book, you can easily craft a series of messages without being repetitive. I'd recommend that as you go through this book and build your emails, you use the same sequence each time. That way, you will never have to worry if you sent the same one already.

I encourage you to repeat this cycle <u>at least three times</u> for new high value prospects.

Yesware, fantastic app that tracks what happens to your emails after you click send, lets you track which of your emails are most opened and replied to; it also tells you when an email has been opened, so you know when to follow up. They have an enormous amount of data about sales emails which have been sent. After analyzing 500,000 emails sent by their users in a single quarter of 2014, they found something interesting:

1. If your email is EVER going to get opened, it happens within a day of sending it 91% of the time.
2. 90% of replies to emails happen within the first day after they were opened.

Knowing that, you know that if your email hasn't been opened within 24 hours, don't count on it getting opened… so it's time to follow up. On the other hand, if your email has been opened, you can give it another day for a reply. After that, you know it's likely not coming… and it's time for another follow-up.

They also found that if an email goes unanswered, a second email nets a 21% chance of getting a reply, and the odds of getting a reply increases if you keep sending. In fact, until email number nine the odds don't dip below double digits. If you mix calls in between your emails, you'll increase your chances even further.

EMAIL COMMANDMENT # 6:

Email Often. Most People Under Email, Not Over

In Appendix B, I discuss a number of my favorite email tools; there you'll find a link to where the generous folks at Yesware have offered you two months, free of charge, if you want to try their service out.

In case you are curious my own prospecting sequence goes like this:

1) Call and email #1
2) Call and email #2
3) Email #3
4) Email #4
5) Call and email #5
6) Email #6

For a copy of the complete Brilliant Call Openers Guide that takes you step by step through crafting the best openers for your sales conversations simply register this book by going to Bonus.The10SecondSale.com and enter your email and the code "opener" to get all the free resources from the book.

Or you can text "#opener" to 1 (708) 221-9627 to have just the checklist emailed to you. We'll text you right back to ask for your email to send it to.

Subject Line Strategies

A huge part of getting your email read lies in your subject line; having a lousy subject line practically ensures your email won't ever get read. Remember, your target probably gets 200+ emails a day. If they work an eight-hour day (eight hours of actual work), that means they need to read, process and respond to 25 emails every hour, doing nothing else all day. This makes it impossible for most people to actually properly handle and consider every email that they get.

How do they decide what to read?

So, how do they decide which ones get read, in what order and which get trashed without even being given a second glance? Everybody has their own method, but there are a couple of general rules of thumb which most people follow.

As most of us go through our inbox, we scan it for a couple things. Most people look at who the message is from. Those from people we deem very important get read first. This includes emails from people bosses, spouseses, kids or people from whom we were waiting for replies.

Once those emails are read and dealt with, then we move on to looking at subject lines. It's important to keep that in mind as you are crafting your subject line; we analyze the subject line along with considering who the message is from. So naturally, a message with the subject "Get a FREE weight loss assessment" from someone you don't know gets trashed without reading. The same message from your physician, who told you the week before that you were going to die of a heart attack within one year if you didn't lose 25 pounds, gets read right away. Your level of relationship with the sender will in part determine how likely it is that it gets read. If you do not already have a strong relationship with the recipient, ask yourself how you would respond to an email with the subject line you are using.

Before you decide to fire off the email thinking that you are okay with the subject line based on your existing relationship with the person, consider one more thing. Just because someone is a subscriber on your list and gets regular emails from you, that does not mean they read every one of your emails. If most of the emails which someone gets from you are broadcast emails of newsletters, affiliate offers, content marketing or really any sort of frequent broadcasts, consider that even though they know who you are, they may low-prioritize your emails.

Many people skip over most of the emails from frequent senders. If that's you, it's even more critical to nail your subject line. Do not assume that because you use a different from: address on those emails that they don't lump that email and your personal email address into one category of "You". Here's one tip that I learned from a client who is a frequent sender: when he sends me something that he wants to ensure that I realize is different, his subject line starts [PERSONAL, NOT BROADCAST]. When I scan my emails looking for the "who's it from" / "what's it about" combination, those stand out and don't get classified with his broadcasts.

How do I get my email read?

In order to help get your email read, you need to keep in mind what is the primary goal of your email. In the case of a sales email, your most common goals will be to a) get a conversation started with the person, or b) get a reply. The goal is not to make the email easy to find when searching, it's not to make it super clear what the email is about. You want them to read the email and act on it.

You'll want the email to be clear, to the point and to generate interest or curiosity.

What's a bad subject line? Anything that does not get opened. It's also one that does not convey any meaning, value or curiosity. Here are some examples of really bad subject lines for sales emails (these are all ones that I've received personally). Some of these may be okay subject lines if you are sending a non-sales email to a friend, but none are even remotely okay in a sales email... especially when sending to someone you don't already have a good relationship with.

Here are some examples of particularly bad subject lines:

- **Greetings** - This means literally nothing to me. Lots of other emails will grab my attention instead.
- **Hello** - Again, if I don't know you, this means nothing. It does not make me curious.
- **A question** - If I don't know you, why would I care about your question?
- **Coffee?** - I don't know you and you start the conversation by asking for what would be probably a minimum of one hour of my time (including travel, shifting mindset in and out of the office, etc.)... No, I don't think so.
- **Hi** - Really? It won't matter that your email message is compelling; I'll probably never get to it.
- **Help** - Who are you?

- **Can you help me?** - I've barely got time to read my emails, let alone help someone I don't know.
- **Can we meet?** - Asking for a time commitment before you have established value is not going to get you anywhere.
- Or worse yet, an email with no subject line at all.

To get read and replied to, your subject line needs to be interesting. To do that while remaining professional, there are a three things which work really well.

1) Clearly convey the point of the message and show something interesting or valuable. This works really well when you were referred to the person or you have some inside information from a contact, your research or something they requested from you or your company. For example, if they requested your special report on boosting engagement on their Facebook page, you could and should reference that in the subject line. Try something like:

I've got another Facebook engagement strategy for you.

That gets you past the "I don't know this person" filter by directly relating to something they are interested in.

Alternatively, if you've been referred by a contact of theirs, you could say:

Bob Lynch suggested I get in touch.

That gets you past the same filter by leveraging Bob Lynch's name instead.

2) Ask a question.

Tony Robbins teaches our minds are programmed to answer questions. If you ask yourself a question like "Why does this always happen to me?" Your mind is going to supply an answer, even if it's not helpful. This same phenomenon is useful in subject lines. When you ask a question in a subject line, their mind wants to answer it. It draws them to your email, and often to at least read the first couple of sentences. If your email is short, to the point and conveys value to them, that's all you need.

3) Start a sentence in the subject line, but don't finish it.

This one is a bit controversial. It shows up on some lists of things not to do in email. In the course of regular correspondence with someone, I'd agree. That approach can be a bit annoying. The reason that it is annoying is the exact reason why you want to use it sometimes. Your brain does not like the incomplete thought and wants to finish the sentence; it almost compels your reader to look at the email body. That's exactly what you want. Just be don'tover use it with the same reader. I recommend only using that tactic once or twice in an email sequence. You can make this even more powerful by combining it with approach number two, asking a question. Start a question in the subject line, but don't finish it until the body of the email.

The best words for your subject line

The folks at Yesware analyze lots of email statistics. With over half a million emails sent by their users every quarter, they have a lot of data to work with. Combining some of their research and my own experience, I've compiled a list of 30 individual words for subject lines which statistically get the best reply rates.

Unlike a marketing email where you want someone to read the email and click a link, with a sales email, you want an actual reply from them; as such, I culled this list from those subjects with the highest replies, not opens.

Steps	Follow	Trial
Campaign	New	Can
Date	Listing	One
Update	Quick	Time
Renewal	Meeting	Email
Next	Day	Information
Executive	Best	World
Intro	Account	Just
Call	Contact	Get
Introduction	Question	Mobile

Getting ready to email

Before you start typing, there are a couple things which you will want to do.

Firstly (and in fact, you should do this before you modify any of the templates that are to come later in the book), you need to clearly know and be able to articulate what it is that you do. You need to know and be able to clearly articulate as many of the results you create for your customers. You need to know, understand and be able to briefly describe why your customers buy from you.

Do you even know what you are selling?

When most people read that, they probably think "Okay, no problem. I got that down cold!" The truth is, you may not. In fact, when I ask people what they sell or what they do, most get it wrong. Let me say that again... most people don't even answer the question about what they do correctly! Those who do often take multiple paragraphs before they get the idea across, but for the purpose of creating email sequences you'll need to have multiple succinct answers to those questions.

I often hear business owners talking about what they do by describing what they're selling. They may say, "I'm a chiropractor; I provide chiropractic services," "I cure backaches," "I'm a marketing consultant," or "I help companies get more leads." There's an old sales adage which goes something like: "Don't sell them the drill; you need to sell them the hole."

What that means is that you need to think in terms of having someone in an aisle of the hardware store, looking at a bunch of drills; they're not really there to buy a drill, yet most of the sales reps which come up to them in that aisle in their hardware store are going to try to sell them a drill. Why they're really there is because they need to make a hole. Therefore, you should sell them the hole and focus on how easy it will be to make one if you use a particular drill or a particular set of bits versus others, and how clean the hole will be, etc.

That's ultimately what you're selling. This approach, though, still misses the mark; it misses the mark because no one wants a bunch of holes in their wall. That's not really what they're after. What they really want is to hang a shelf on the wall where they're going to put pictures of their family from various vacations that they've been on for the last half a dozen years, and they want to ensure that when the cat jumps on that shelf, the shelf does not fall down and hit their six-month-old child on the head. That's what they really want.

In that sales situation, if you focus on selling a drill, maybe you're going to get a sale for the cheapest drill in that aisle. If you talk about the holes, yes, you'll sell a slightly better drill and probably with a good set of drill bits. But if you focus on what customer really wants and sell them that, then you're going to talk about an additional option, which is the installation service, where you're going to send a guy from the store out to their house with all of the appropriate hardware to make sure that the shelf is put up properly; it's going to be sturdy; it's not going to fall; it's going to be level and straight, so nothing is going to roll off of it.

While you're there, you may have other punch job

items that you get to take care for that family as well. You end up with a much more profitable sale.

I had a conversation with a client recently. He is a marketing consultant in Chicago and he's really good at what he does. He was, however, having difficulty setting up new appointments with prospects. In particular, he had started attending a number of local business meetings in an attempt to make new contacts and schedule appointments. He was about to give up on that tactic. Even going to these meetings one to three times a week for the last two months, he hadn't scheduled a single appointment yet.

We did a little role-playing so I could understand how these conversations were going. We started out and I asked him "What do you do?" He replied, "I'm a marketing consultant."

I quickly saw the problem. I decided to play with him a little bit and asked "So what?" He looked at me a little quizzically and was obviously taken aback by my reply. Obviously, in a real-world situation, no one would actually ask that… but many people would be thinking it.

So, I explained to him that what I'm really looking for is a brief explanation of what he actually does for his clients. I saw the light bulb go on; he smiled and then went into a two-and-a-half-minute long explanation of what he actually does. I consider myself to have a high degree of impatience, probably more so than most, but two and a half minutes would be more than enough for most people to lose interest.

I took him through the exercise I'll show you in a minute, and after just a little bit of practice and planning, he went off to his next business meet-up. I got a call from him the very next day; he was incredibly excited because he had booked three new meetings with prospects, just at that one single meet-up. He's continued to use that method to meet new clients and actually averages two appointments now for every one of these events he attends.

What you do sell:

This same exercise will give you some great insights into your own business that you can use on cold calls, warm calls, introductory emails, marketing materials and anywhere else that you may be interacting with new potential leads.

The first step of this exercise is to come up with as many ways to describe what you do. Sit down with a blank sheet of paper and think about what you do. Write down each thing you come up with; you should be able to come up with 20 to 30, or even more. If you are a marketing consultant, you might have items on your list about getting your clients found, improving their rankings on search engines, improving the number of leads a client gets, increasing foot traffic, managing social media, etc.

Here is a formula you can use to word that statement:

> We (specialize in / help / advise / assist / guide / support / work with)
> (type of industry, person or company you are calling) who are
> (a specific problem / a specific hot button they will likely have) while / as well as (a specific benefit they receive when they use you)

Step two is to brainstorm all the words and phrases which describe what you do. If you were calling on behalf of a computer reseller you might come up with:

- We are a business computer company.
- We manage and install corporate IT solutions
- We keep corporate IT systems running smoothly
- We provide business technology solutions.

The more ways you have of describing what you do, the more ways you have of being able to connect to potential clients.

The third step is to put together as many statements as you can which build credibility about your business. You want to have a number ways to explain why they should believe you can do what you say. Your prospect doesn't know if you are just some guy in their parent's garage, or any better than the other 20 people who email and call every day, or even as good as the first five links they'll get if they Google your benefit statement.

Here are some examples of what you might come up with:

- Worked with over 2,500 clients
- Helped 476 businesses in the Houston area
- Over 2.5 billion burgers served
- Manufactures like IBM, Apple, and Dell use us
- We've been rated the number one company at XXXX in the area
- We helped double the lead conversions of our last customer in Bloomingdale in less than 90 days.
- Over 167 books have been published and reached bestseller-status using our system in the last 120 days alone.

One key to nailing your credibility statement is to be specific. Don't be general.

Step four (and the final step) in this exercise is to craft as many ways as possible to describe the benefits you bring to your clients. This is perhaps the most important part. You must clearly, quickly and specifically tell them what benefit they can expect from talking to you. The stronger the benefit you can articulate, the more likely it is that they will speak with you.

Brainstorm as many of these as possible.

Write down every benefit you bring to the table; write down every reason why people buy from you, write down every single one that you can think of, come up with everything you can. Keep brainstorming until you have a list of at least 20, but it would be ideal if you could come up with a list of 30 to 40 items.

Then, when you think you've exhausted everything, ask some of your customers why they chose you (you may be surprised that they have reasons you'd never even thought of).

Here are some examples:
- We reduce IT downtime by 50%
- We ensure that your servers never experience more than four hours of downtime
- We reduce IT system maintenance costs by 72%

Some generic examples:
- Decrease cost of X by Y%
- Reduce X usage by Y%
- Increase revenue by X%

As you narrow down your list to your final choices, do not list one of the benefits as being your cost; don't say that you are lower cost than anyone else, that you are inexpensive, cheap or that you save them money on your service. If you enter your first conversation with a statement about your low pricing, you will spend the entire relationship with them re-negotiating your price every time a competitor mentions they can meet or beat your price.

As a guiding principle, keep in mind that the benefit statement should be simple and direct. It should be a benefit. Do not embellish it with fluff words like "best", "superior" or "faster". People don't know enough at this point to be able to agree or disagree... it's just your opinion and you haven't generated the trust yet for them to accept that.

Know your target

It's not always enough to have great benefits and credibility. It's also important that you   make sure that you take the time to learn something about your prospect, especially if it's potentially a high value contact. These days, this is pretty easy to get in the head of your target. In just a few minutes, you can read their blog, their LinkedIn profile and posts, check out their Twitter feed, find out about them on their company website and check out their Facebook profile. You can learn about their interests, positions on certain issues and their career and personal background. It's fairly easy these days to find out a prospect's career background, what they read, what they do on weekends, who their favorite bloggers, authors and movies are as well as if you have common acquaintances or friends. As you'll see in the email templates, these details can often be used as part of your approach.

Let them know you

Don't forget that just as you can do research on your prospect, they can do the same on you. Often, before replying to your email, your prospect will do the same thing to you, by checking out you and your company online. Are you prepared for that?

Do you have a solid LinkedIn profile? Have you made your articles, books or podcasts known? Is your Facebook profile public and full of pictures of you that you wouldn't want your prospects to see? Make sure that you

have built out your LinkedIn profile and that you have

adjusted the privacy settings of your Facebook profile (or

at least have your postings able to stand up to professional

scrutiny).

Final Checklist

Before you send your email, also take a pass through this checklist for "10-Second Sales Emails". Run through and make sure you've covered everything here before you hit send. This all may seem like a lot, but once you've gotten the hang of it and customized the templates for your own use, you'll be getting emails done in just over 10 seconds.

- ✓ WIIFM... What's in it for me? The email has to appeal to what they might get out of interacting with you. If it just tells them that you are smart, cool, talented and awesome, they will not be impressed.

- ✓ SO WHAT? Does it pass the "So what?" test? When they read about what you do, will they have to ask "So what?" or will it be immediately obvious to them? You want them fascinated, involved, excited and ready to talk to you about it more.

- ✓ Is the writing BORING? The number one cause of boring emails is leaving out WIIFM and SO WHAT.

- ✓ Are you keeping the email to 220 words or less? Remember to keep it short.

- ✓ Are you mixing up the FORMATTING in a way which keeps it easy to read?

✓ Are you throwing in lists of bullet points to mix up the pace and break up the look of the email?

✓ Have you researched your prospect and included something you found in the email?

✓ Are you using action verbs to keep the momentum rolling? Are you sure? Go back through and check one more time.

✓ Are you using specifics? REAL time, place, people and numbers in your benefit and credibility statements?

✓ Did you read it OUT LOUD one final time?

✓ Have you included a call to action?

✓ Are you presenting the price? If so, and you are not already at the present-a-solution-stage of the sales process, take it out. You want commitment for conversation at this point. Don't refer yet to your price, discounts or compare your pricing to competition.

✓ Have you established credibility in the email?

✓ Are you using jargon that they may not understand?

✓ Have you given them a reason to respond NOW?

✓ Is your email believable? Did you exaggerate or include unbelievable claims?

✓ Do you get to the point right away?

✓ Have you read it through and tried to cut out the excess words?

✓ Are you enthusiastic about what you're selling? That little bit of personality always comes through.

✓ Did you double check that the time zones you refer to are in THEIR time zone?

✓ Is your email EASY to read?

For a copy of the complete Brilliant Call Openers Guide that takes you step by step through crafting the best openers for your sales conversations simply register this book by going to Bonus.The10SecondSale.com and enter your email and the code "opener" to get all the free resources from the book.

Or you can text "#opener" to 1 (708) 221-9627 to have just the checklist emailed to you. We'll text you right back to ask for your email to send it to.

Using the templates

In the next section of the book, you'll have get over 40 of my favorite email templates.

In this section, you'll find the emails in a slightly different font each followed by some notes about how to use and customize the template.

In each email there is some text surrounded by square brackets "**[replace this text]**." Hopefully it should be obvious what to replace the text in those brackets with. It'll usually be something like the prospects name, what they do, your name, or something like that.

For much of the text I debated how plug and play to make the emails. For example, I could have put "[put your benefit statement here]" to make it as obvious about what goes where. After much debate though I decided it would be more beneficial for you to see actual emails that have been used successfully so you'd have something to model. In order to do that though I had to assume, you'd be able to figure out to replace my sample text with your own.

In these templates you'll need to replace benefits,

times, what you do, etc with the text in the emails before you send them.

Oh, and one final note. When you replace "[Contact Info]" with your contact info, keep it simple. You want it to be easy to read on any device (including a phone) and for them to not get distracted by links to your FaceBook Profile, LinkedIn Page, Twitter Account, etc.. Simply include your name, company, phone and email.

Download every template from this book right into your favorite email program or editor. Simply register this book by going to Bonus.The10SecondSale.com and enter your email and the code "templates" to get all the free resources from the book.

Or you can text "#templates" to 1 (708) 221-9627 to have just the checklist emailed to you. We'll text you right back to ask for your email to send it to.

Prospecting Templates

Prospecting is crucial to your sales. Before you say to yourself that you don't do prospecting, or cold calling, lets be clear that prospecting is NOT the same thing as cold calling. Here are a couple quick definitions for you.

Cold Call = Calling someone whom you have never met, has no idea who you are or what you do, and has not done anything to express interest in you our what you have to offer.

Prospect = Someone who is in your target demographic or who you want to sell (or attempt to sell) your services to. You have not yet spoken with about it one on one and they have not done anything to express interest to you yet.

Lead = Someone who is in your target demographic, and has expressed interest in what you offer. They may have filled out a form on your website, called your office, or listened to your info video.

Prospecting = Any sales related activities that lead towards getting your first person to person conversation with a prospect or lead.

Since prospecting is all about getting that first sales conversation going, every business needs to consistently engage in prospecting activities. In fact, one of my favorite sales tips is: ABP (Always Be Prospecting)

It's one of the most important part of the sales process. No matter how effectively you automate your marketing and sales process, at some point you will need to talk to potential customers. Prospecting does not necessarily mean cold calling. It is a combination of your activities that lead to conversations with new potential clients. Outbound calling and emailing to warm leads is still prospecting.

No matter how much business you are working on now, you should make time at least every week (ideally every day) to prospect. If you don't do that and keep your pipeline of possible opportunities overfull you will be unhappily surprised when you finish your current projects and don't have enough paying clients. That whipsaw can be quit quick too. I once went from a $29k commission check on month to barely $2k the next because I ignored my prospecting efforts for too long and closed a huge portion of my pipeline all at once.

This section contains a number of emails you can use in your prospecting efforts.

The prospecting templates that follow have been broken up into 3 categories.

Cold Prospecting - Use these emails when reaching out to a prospect who you have not spoken to, not met and has not requested information from you. This is for prospect you want to start a dialogue with, but have not yet done so.

Warm Prospecting - These emails are useful for contacting leads whom you have had some contact with, but you really have not started the sales process with. They could have requested information from your website, met you at an event, or attended an event you were hosting or speaking at.

Universal Prospecting - The Universal emails are useful as part of your prospecting sequence once you have already reached out using the Cold or Warm emails and not yet connected with them.

Cold Prospecting

Cold Email Referencing a Common Contact

Hi, [prospect name],

We are both acquainted with [share contact name].

I saw from your website that you do [what they do]. I am contacting you because I have some ideas about generating more sales for you.

Instant Customer has a software platform that helps companies get found on line more often, convert 27-87% more of your web visitors into solid leads, and ultimately convert a more of your leads into customers.

I would be happy to share a few strategies with you that should improve your web conversions. If the strategies makes sense to you and you indicate you'd like help implementing them we can also talk about how Instant Customer may be able to help you. Even if you don't utilize our software I am sure these strategies will be helpful for your online strategy.

I have 15-20 minutes by phone available
Tuesday at 10:15. Will that work for you?
If not let me know a time in the next few
days that does.

I look forward to hearing from you.

All the best,

[Your Name]

[Contact Info]

NOTES

- Notice that I simply state we are both acquainted with. I'm not saying this person referred me to them, just simply that we both know them. This works very well for reaching out to people whom you are a 2nd level connection with on LinkedIn or on Facebook. It establishes (regardless of how remote) a common connection with the reader. Possible places you can find points of commonality include:

  - Career background or course
  - Details of their job
  - Personal interests including what they read, do on weekends, favorite books, articles, movies and other cultural interests.
  - Relationship status (married people with kids, vs single moms think about things differently)
  - Mutual contacts from Facebook or LinkedIn

- Quickly get to the point and establishing specific result you can provide. Use specific #s when you can.

- Offer to share ways to improve their business with them. Let them know you'll only pitch them afterwards and if they want.

- The email tells them you want to talk, and offers a specific time. A busy person can read this email in 30 seconds, decide that they want to talk and simply reply "yes". It makes it easy for them to agree.

Cold Email Referencing a Commonality

Hi, [prospect name],

I noticed on your LinkedIn profile that you are active in Rotary International. As a result my son is actually a beneficiary of your service. He has received some vision aids from Rotary and attends their camp for the blind every summer.

I am contacting you because I have some ideas about generating more sales for you.

Instant Customer has a software platform that helps companies get found on line more often, convert 27-87% more of your web visitors into solid leads, and ultimately convert a more of your leads into customers.

I would be happy to share a few strategies with you that should improve your web conversions. If the strategies make sense to you and you indicate you'd like help implementing them we can also talk about how Instant Customer may be able to help you. Even if you don't utilize our software I am sure these strategies will be helpful for your online strategy.

I have 15-20 minutes by phone available

Tuesday at 10:15. Will that work for you? If not let me know a time in the next few days that does.

I look forward to hearing from you.

All the best,

[Your Name]

[Contact Info]

NOTES

- Possible places you can find points of commonality include:

  - Career background or course
  - Details of their job
  - Personal interests including what they read, do on weekends, favorite books, articles, movies and other cultural interests.
  - Relationship status (married people with kids, vs single moms think about things differently)
  - Mutual contacts from Facebook or LinkedIn

- Quickly get to the point and establishing specific result you can provide. Use specific #s when you can.

- Offer to share ways to improve their business with them. Let them know you'll only pitch them afterwards and if they want.

- The email tells them you want to talk, and offers a specific time. A busy person can read this email in 30 seconds, decide that they want to talk and simply reply "yes". It makes it easy for them to agree.

Cold Email with a Solid Reference

Subject Line: [Reference name] suggested we get in touch.

Hi [prospect name],

[Reference name], recommended that I contact you. My name is David Traub and I'm the Sales and Marketing Strategist at Instant Customer.

I read the article about in Crain's about your recent expansion. Congratulations! I've been through a rapid expansion myself recently and I think there could be an opportunity to share some great ideas.

Do you have time for a 10-minute phone call? If so, would one of these times work?

- Wednesday anytime in the afternoon

- Thursday at 2:15 EST?

- Friday anytime after 11:30 EST and before 3:45 EST

If those times don't work let me know something that does and I'll find a way to make it work.

Let me know what # to call you on, or if you'd prefer my direct line is (847) xxx-

xxxx

Thanks,

[Your Name]

[Contact Info]

NOTES

- Only use a true reference when you say someone recommended you contact them! Do not try to stretch it there. If you just know the reference, but they didn't recommend you contact the person, then use the Cold Email referencing a common contact template instead. You will kill any deal or relationship you establish with both your prospect and your reference if you do.

- Quickly introduce your referral and who you are.

- Introduce a topic for a call or meeting quickly. Do not linger on it. One quick statement is enough. Any longer and you risk boring the person and they will quit reading.

- Request a SHORT amount of time. Busy people are less likely to say yes to longer time commitments.

- Offer a couple time choices for them.

- Offer the time choices with time zone spelled out and USE THEIR timezone. Do the translation yourself, don't make them do it. See the

recommended resources for a great time zone chart

you should have posted in your work area.

EMAIL COMMANDMENT # 7:

Always use their Time Zone when referencing a time of day

Cold introduction Using a Trigger Event

[Lead's first name],

I saw the article on your website today about your entering a new market. It looks like an exciting time for your company.

As you start your expansion, are you intending on using your website for lead generation? If so, one think you may want to consider is to put a call to action button and link at the bottom of every article. Have that link direct to a page or a form that they can fill out to get some free information. It can be a training video, a PDF of a white paper… Anything really that might be of interest to those who liked the article.

That way you gain a way for them to become a lead in your system and get their contact details. When we made that change on our site we increased our lead flow right away by 126%.

I have a couple other suggestions I'd be glad to share with you that I believe could help. Do you have 10-15 minutes to connect later this week. I have time Wednesday at 3:15 EST, Thursday from 10:15am to 2:15PM, or Friday at 1:45.

If those times don't work let me know something that does and I'll find a way to make it work.

Let me know what # to call you on, or if you'd prefer my direct line is (847) xxx-xxxx

Thanks,

[Your Name]

[Contact Info]

NOTES

- Like the above examples, keep it short and introduce a clear way that you can help the prospect's company.

- Request a SHORT amount of their time. Busy people are MUCH less likely to say yes the longer you are asking for.

- Offer a couple time choices for them.

- Offer the time choices with time zone spelled out and USE THEIR timezone. Do the translation yourself, don't make them do it. See the recommended resources for a great time zone chart you should have posted in your work area.

Completely Cold Email

Subject : Interested in chatting about lead conversions

Hi [prospect name],

My name is David and I'm the Sales and Marketing Strategist at Instant Customer. I came across your website the other day and was intrigued.

My guess is that right now, 3 of [prospect's company's name] biggest concerns right now are:

1. Converting free members to paid customers

2. Increasing sign ups for your trial service

3. Escalating your paid subscribers to higher service levels

Recently we finished a project at [another customer] where we helped one customer increase their trial sign ups by 247% and increased his trail to customer conversion rates by 28%. Another client just doubled the # of her members that switched into her private client program.

I'd love to chat with you and share 2 of

the key strategies they implemented that
helped them do that.

Do you have 15-20 minutes to meet Thursday
at 10:15 or Friday at 2:45.

All the best,

[Your Name]

[Contact Info]

NOTES

- Quickly get to the point.

- List 2 to 3 problems that you have been proven to fix

- Document 1 or 2 relevant successes

- Offer to share the strategies with them.

- Offer time suggestions to make it easy for them to say yes if one works.

Completely Cold Email 2

Subject : Appropriate person

Hi [prospect name],

I am writing to you in the hopes that you can point me to the appropriate person who is responsible for your sales team. I also wrote to [Person 2] and [Person 3] for feedback as well.

[Your benefit intro goes here. As an example…] Sell Brilliantly helps professional service organizations double or triple their lead conversion rate while increasing average fess. We've done this for over 150 companies in the Chicago area.

If you are the appropriate person to speak with, do you have 15-20 minutes to talk Thursday at 10:15 or Friday at 2:45. If not, who do you recommend I talk to?

All the best,

[Your Name]

[Contact Info]

NOTES

- The subject line of "appropriate person" works to create curiosity at the same time that it directly communicates what you are writing about.

- The first sentence jumps directly to why you are writing, yet should be slightly vague to keep them curious and reading.

- Reference at least one person who is likely above them in the company organization. People have a tendency to respond if they think you may connect with their boss. At the same time by targeting a level or two above who you may normally target, you may actually get a response from up the food chain. They higher you are selling to in the organization, the better off you always are.

- Don't reference more than 3 people other wise it seems like you may be spamming the company.

- Send the same email to each person on your list separately and change up the names you listed. Response rates are higher if you send separate emails.

- List 2 to 3 problems that you have been proven to fix

- Document 1 or 2 relevant successes

- Use the same general formula for your benefit intro here as you would in a great call opener.

- Offer time suggestions to make it easy for them to say yes if one works.

For a copy of the complete Brilliant Call Openers Guide that takes you step by step through crafting the best openers for your sales conversations simply register this book by going to Bonus.The10SecondSale.com and enter your email and the code "opener" to get all the free resources from the book.

Or you can text "#opener" to 1 (708) 221-9627 to have just the checklist emailed to you. We'll text you right back to ask for your email to send it to.

Warm Prospecting

What Is

Subject : What is …

Hi [prospect name],

Thanks for attending our LiveCast yesterday on leaving great voicemail messages. My name is David and I'm the Sales and Marketing Strategist at Instant Customer.

What is your reason for interest in this topic?

All the best,

[Your Name]

[Contact Info]

NOTES

- It's critical that you leave the subject line as is for this email. Don't get creative, and DON'T make it a complete sentence. It's important for a couple reasons. 1) it makes it stand out. It's different than everything else they are getting, and 2) your brain does not like an incomplete question. When the prospect sees it they know you are asking something and automatically want to know what the question is, thus it's likely to get opened.

- Use this email when the lead is warm. They have done something to raise their hand and let you know they are interested and reference that in the first sentence.

- This email is powerful for a couple reasons. First of all, you'll get a number of responses back from people who clearly let you know they aren't interested and thought it was something else, or that their sister signed them up, or whatever. You could have wasted 2-4 attempts to contact them by phone for this. Secondly, the leads with the most interest and urgency will be raising their hand with more information and calling attention to themselves. If you send this email immediately after a webinar or live cast you'll quickly find out which 10% of the leads not to bother with, and which 10% are likely your hottest leads.

- Keep the email as brief as the example. It helps cut through the clutter, and makes it easy for the prospect to respond.

- This email can be used after a webinar or live cast, after a trade show, after a presentation you gave, or in response to an inbound lead.

Email to an Inbound Lead

Subject : Your question about voicemails

[Lead name].

Hi, it's David from Sell Brilliantly. Yesterday you requested information on how to leave a great voicemail message that gets you return calls. I took a look at your website to understand more about what you do, and I have a few tips and suggestions that you can use.

When do you have 15-20 minutes in the next couple days to go over them?

All the best,

[Your Name]

[Contact Info]

NOTES

- Do this in manually in addition to any auto-responder that goes out. While you may have a great auto-responder sequence that you use, you want to send this one manually as well because some people's Spam protection will automatically catch your auto-emails. Others will skip over or ignore those messages as well since they a) aren't personal to them, and b) are likely much longer and harder to read than this simple email and call to action.

- As an inbound lead they have already indicated interest in what you offer or had to say, this capitalizes on that interest by providing an personalized level of service.

- Part of what is different here is that you are offering your own help or advice, you aren't trying to hammer them with hard sell or hyped up emails to get them to buy. You are showing you want to establish a connection with them. It's simple, and by asking for time suggestions you'll find a lot of your leads will schedule time with you rather than you having to try calling them multiple times to catch them.

- Again the hottest leads tend to push themselves to the top of your follow up list this way.

Email Someone You Met at an Event

Subject : Quick Steps to get the most out of your Publish & Profit workshop

[Lead name].

Hi, it's David from Instant Customer. Thanks for attending the Publish and Profit Live event. I hope you found the sessions interesting and useful. Even more important I hope you came away with some good ideas for integrating the book leverage into your business.

I would be happy to do a short 20 minute next steps review with you to evaluate you've got the highest value action items queued up to work on.

When do you have 15-20 minutes in the next couple days to keep the momentum going?

All the best,

[Your Name]

[Contact Info]

NOTES

- This email is good for establishing one on one contact with people you met in person.

- You can tweak this email to use either if you were part of the company putting on the event, or simply for other attendees that you met and could be good prospects or partners for you.

- Change the beginning to fit your business, the event you met at and what you can do for them.

- Again the hottest leads tend to push themselves to the top of your follow up list this way.

Email someone You Met at an Event 2

Subject : Met you at the Chicago Salesforce Users Group - Short Baldish Guy with the Cool Fedora

Hi [Lead name],

Hi, it's David from Sell Brilliantly. We met at the Salesforce group in Chicago last week. I'm the guy who helps optimize your Salesforce system so your sales reps actually want to use it because they see it makes them money. It was a pleasure meeting you, and I wanted to follow up on our chat.

You mentioned that ABC Box has invested heavily in Salesforce, but your reps just don't want to use it. That's a common problem and one we love solving. It's often relatively simple to do also. Check out the attachment — I think you'll find it interesting.

I'd be glad to do a 20 minute review of your system with you and give you some direction to get the data you need out of your reps heads and into the system. Can we setup a call this week? I can call you on Wednesday in the afternoon, or almost any time on Thursday. When do you have 20 minutes in the next couple days?

All the best,

[Your Name]

[Contact Info]

NOTES

- This email is particularly good when you've had a decent conversation with the prospect at an event.

- Reference yourself in the subject line in the way they will likely remember you. Don't call yourself the Salesforce Implementation Guru if what they'll remember first is the awesome hat you were wearing. You may find that even if you are sending this email to 5 people you met that your subject will change for each based on something that stood out in your particular conversation.

- Quickly remind them of where you met, and why he should care. This is where you'll remind him of what you want to be known for with him.

- In the case of a prospect where you already had a good conversation with them at an event, sending an attachment that is short and CLEARLY highlights what they prospect is looking for is acceptable.

- Again the hottest leads tend to push themselves to

the top of your follow up list this way.

Another Event Email

Subject : Your Website Assessment

Hi [Lead name],

Hi, it's David from Instant Customer. Thanks again for attending Convert Conference. Per my previous voicemail, I am reaching out to schedule your one-on-one website consultation.

During this free call, our Marketing Strategist will discuss concrete strategies you can easily implement on your website to generate two to three times as many inbound leads from your site.

We offer these sessions for free because many companies start to see the value in working with us to improve their lead acquisition and conversions. Even if you don't want to continue working with us, you'll get a huge amount of value from the information you learn on your site consultation.

If you are interested in generating more leads from your website without having to increase your advertising spend, please send me a few times in the next week that would work for your session.?

All the best,

[Your Name]

[Contact Info]

NOTES

- Like some of the other templates, this email teases them with direct assistance to their situation.

- Update the email with details of where they met you or your team, and what you can do for them.

- As usual keep it short, and end with a clear call to action.

Universal Prospecting

Email with Voicemail

Subject: Voicemail

[Lead name],

I just left you a voicemail as well.

I was calling about your lead conversion rates. I just finished helping a client increase the conversions of leads from his website by an additional 20% in less than 30 days.

After reviewing your website I think the same 2 strategies would likely help you. Do you have 10 minutes available by phone later this week so that I can share those strategies with you?

I'm available all of Tuesday afternoon or Wednesday morning. What would work for you?

All the best,

[Your Name]

[Contact Info]

NOTES

- Like the earlier examples, be brief and to the point.

- Mention your voicemail that you left

- Give them a clear concise benefit you have produced

- Offer to share with them. Don't try to pitch your services, simply offer them something. What you want at this point is the conversation, not the sale. Don't try to do too much all at once.

- Be generous with the time you have available yet. You've not established yet a right to be restrictive with your time since you are reaching out to them cold.

Reactivate a Stalled Lead

Subject: Your interest in Sell Brilliantly

Hi [lead name],

I noticed that you've visited our website a few times and downloaded our Questions Report on the best 25 questions your sales people should be asking, but probably aren't. I've reviewed your website and have some suggestions on how you can tailor some of those questions for your business.

Sell Brilliantly offers a 30 minute sales assessment where we can review those tips and more suggestions that you can implement today to improve your sales conversions, spend less time with tire kickers, and close more business faster than you thought possible.

When do you have a few minutes to connect?

All the best,

[Your Name]

[Contact Info]

NOTES

- This email is also short, sweet and to the point.

- It mentions something specific about their interest (use this when you know details about their visit)

- Offer something particularly helpful. A 30 minute assessment really is a 30 minute sales discovery call, but they can easily provide value on their own to your prospect.

When Prospecting Email is Ignored
Subject:

Hi [lead name],

I've tried to reach you a few times about converting more sales leads into appointments. Do you have a few minutes to connect today or sometime this week? If so, when's a good time to talk?

All the best,

[Your Name]

[Contact Info]

NOTES

- This email is also short, sweet and to the point.

- Resist the temptation to put more advantages in the email. Pick one primary and keep it short.

- Send this after you have emailed and called a few times without a response. You'll be supposed how often your messaging will have resonated with them, but they just haven't had a chance to respond. Just a simple, do you have a few minutes gets a surprising response rate.

Dealing with Obstacles

Templates

I probably could have called this section "Getting things unstuck" since the templates mostly have to do with trying to prompt a response from a lead or prospect that went cold. Or for reviving a long dormant contact.

You might wonder why this section is not chock full of answers to various objections. The reason is that objective handling is direct selling. In a 1:1 sales situation your actually selling should be done face to face, over the phone, over Skype, or in some direct real-time communication model. It's critical that you can see and/or hear their reactions, their face and have their complete attention. You do not want to fire of an email with a complex objection response to them when they may actually end up reading while boring a plane and have 3 seconds to comprehend it while at the same time trying to fight the guy behind them for the last open space in the overhead.

When a lead or prospect calls or emails you with an objection, call them back to talk about it. That is not an email appropriate situation. At most send an email acknowledging their concern, and let them you you have an idea to share with them. Then ask when a good time to talk with them is. Only do that though after you have directly tried to reach them.

Most of these templates also deal with getting something unstuck because according to Harvard Business Review 20% of the most common reasons a sale doesn't close is either that no decision is made (the client does nothing), or that the sales cycle stalls out for some reason. Both are essentially simply stuck deals, so over time you'll want various ways of dealing with that.

Kick a deal loose
Subject : Are you...

[Prospect first name],

Are you still looking to improve your sales conversions?

All the best,

[Your Name]

[Contact Info]

NOTES

- Use the subject line of Are you… It begs to be opened and makes them curious.

- Use just 9 words to ask the question. Substitute "sales conversions" with the primary benefit they were interested in.

- DO NOT be tempted to expand on this. The single question with no explanation or reason behind it creates a sort of "open loop" that your lead will find hard to not close.

- I tend to send this about 90 days after they came into my funnel as a lead if there has been no direct contact with them yet or 90 days after they've gone cold with no response if we have talked.

- You will find a surprising % (often as many as 40% or more) will respond to this email. Some will write back with a "no" and explain why… Now you have an objection to work with. For those that say yes, you'll get some ready to move right away, and others will apologize for not responding sooner and explain. The bottom line is that 40-50% of the time you will get the conversation re-started.

Kick a deal loose 2

Subject : Thought you might find this useful…

[Prospect first name],

Are you still looking to increase the number of sales appointments your team sets weekly? Thought you might find this useful: [link to article or reference on related topic]

Would you be available to talk for a few minutes later this week?

[Your Name]

[Contact Info]

NOTES

- Keep the subject line simple, and casual. Like you'd use if you were sending an article to a friend.

- When you send this to a prospect you have talked about use a benefit that was their biggest hot button.

- I tend to send this about 90 days after the first Kick a Deal loose email.

Yet another to Kick Loose
Subject : Active Files

[Prospect first name],

I've just left you a voicemail as well.

I've tried to reach you several times so we can finalize plans for doubling the number of sales appointments your team runs each weeks. Since I haven't heard back from you, I'm going to assume you are no longer interested in doing that and take you out of my active files.

If things change in the future, please feel free to reach out to me at [your contact info].

All the best,

[Your Name]

[Contact Info]

NOTES

- Don't panic about doing this thinking that it seems harsh. It is not. You are not calling them names, blaming them for wasting your time or anything like that.

- Please don't skip the step of leaving the voicemail. A) you may catch them and have a conversation, and B) it amplifies the impact of this message if they get it through multiple mediums.

- This email simply reminds them of the benefit the needed for their business and saying that you are taking them out of your active files. They have no idea what that means, you've intentionally left that out.

- Change up the email so that you are highlighting a very specific result you know they NEEDED.

- DO NOT be tempted to expand on the message. DO NOT offer one last chance or time when you are available to talk. You are intentionally implying that you are taking away their opportunity to work with you for now.

- You will get a surprising number of emails back that say "Wait! Please don't do that. I really need to XXXXX. I've just been super busy. Can you meet sometime next week." You'll actually feel like a school teacher sometimes after sending this email because people will write back and tell you about their cat dying, their husband's aunt's 2nd cousin's gall bladder surgery and more excuses.

- Do not at this point stop considering them a prospect. They should still get your drip marketing, and if the lead was qualified I usually put them back into my call list about 6 months later.

Your Emails were Ignored

Subject : Were lasts month's numbers any better?

Hi [lead name],

I've tried to reach you a few times regarding your interest in improving your sales numbers. However, I have not heard back from you and do not want to be a bother, so I will assume that you are happy with your current sales performance and that improving is not a priority for you at this time.

If this is not the case, and you are still interested, please contact me so that we can discuss how Sell Brilliantly can help you sell smarter, sell better and sell more. You can reach me at [your contact info].

All the best,

[Your Name]

[Contact Info]

NOTES

- This example is great at helping revive a lead that went cold, but does still have interest in what you do.

- This email is a bit more subtle than the previous one, but still quite powerful. I'll typical use this with someone that did not go far enough through my sales process that I have a strong understanding of their specific needs.

Revive an old contact who has gone cold

Subject : I've been thinking about your business and have an idea I'd like to share with you

Hi [lead name],

It has been a while since we talked. I was recently reviewing a sales promotion that a client ran, and it made me think of you. His idea could work brilliantly in your business. He found an immediate 25% increase within 30 days after he did this.

I'd love to share his idea with you. Do you have time Tuesday at 10:30 to talk by phone for 15 minutes?

All the best,

[Your Name]

[Contact Info]

NOTES

- Everyone loves free ideas that made someone else money. Come up with a strong benefit statement that you can use about your prospects primary goal or pain and use it.

- As always, keep the email brief. Ideally they should be able to read the whole thing on their phone without scrolling and reply simply with a yes if the time works for them.

- In this case you are only mentioning 1 time instead of offering a few. This is because a) it's a warm lead who you have already established rapport and value to, and b) you are giving something of value away in addition to giving them your time. In this case you don't have to assume the role of the person with "lower value"

- The purpose of this email is to shake a conversation loose, not pitch something specific in the email. The goal is to get them on the phone and get them talking.

Follow Up Email Templates

Email Someone You Met at an Event
Subject : It was great to

    meet you.

    Hi [lead's first name],

    It was great to meet you at the Chicago Mover's Marketing Conference. I hope you found the sessions interesting and useful and you came away with some good ideas.

    As you may recall I specialize in helping people double the lead flow from their website and as I mentioned I would be happy to do a short (30 minute) review of your website to evaluate it's effectiveness and discuss strategies to

help you get found by qualified
prospects.

Please let me know a good time for
us to connect. I would be happy to
discuss strategies for improving your
website and to tell you more about how
Sell Brilliantly helps you Sell Smarter,
Sell Better and Sell More.

Best Regards,

[Your name]

[Your contact info]

NOTES

- "Meet you." Is the first line of the email, not part of the subject line.

- This email gets opened because people don't like incomplete sentences. They want to know what it was great to...

- Make specific mention of where you met and remind them of your key benefit. If you have multiple reference the one that fits best from what you learned about them at the event.

- This is slightly different than a prospecting email, because I'll use it with someone whom I've already offered the consultation with and wanted to do it.

- Once again you are offering something of value to them, remind them of that.

- As always, keep the email brief. Don't be tempted to start to sell here.

LOU - Letter of Understanding
Subject : Letter of Understanding from
Our Meeting on Wednesday

Hi [lead's first name],

I'm glad we had an opportunity to
meet yesterday.

During the meeting you had indicated
that despite having videos posted on
YouTube you still are finding that you
are getting less than 50 new leads
opting in to your list each month. From
that list, you are getting on average
5-10 of those to agree to a phone call
discovery session and 1-2 actually
closes. Based on your business goals you
need to be generating 5-8 new clients
each month more than you are now. You do
have a limited marketing budget (less
than $1,000) a month, and each new
client generates about $1,500 in revenue
when they come on board with you and are
generally worth a total of $7,000 in
their first year with you and $1,000-
$2,000 each year after that.

You said you are doing 2 new youtube

videos each month. You also do 4-6 meet-ups or small group presentations each month and from those you generally bring in 2-3 new clients each month.

Adding 5-8 additional new clients each month was a priority of 9 out of 10 for you. It was not a lower priority because you need to start cutting back on your hours so that you can spend more time at home with your wife and new son. You barely get to see them now, and 5 new clients a month will give you the additional revenue that you need to hire a competent office manger freeing up your time.

We discussed several methods of increasing your lead-flow and getting more people on your list without having to increase your speaking engagements and only by doing a few more videos each month. Those videos likely will not take more than an extra 1 hour each month to get done. We talked about new systems for ensuring that your list is communicated with regularly and to improve the # of consultation appointment you get from your meet-ups.

You wanted to see more details about how the new marketing plan would work along with costs and discuss them with your partner.

Next Steps:

- I agreed to: put a proposal out for you outlining new strategies and an implementation plan for them. I'll also email you links to 3 client example of before and after from when we updated their campaigns. You'll have the email by Tuesday and I'll have the proposal ready by our next meeting.

- You agreed to: send me by tomorrow your last 3 newsletters, your marketing brochure and the email you send when people join your list. You indicated that if the proposal is within your budget and you and Joanne believe it meets your objectives that you'll be able to decide to move ahead or not at our next meeting. Also you will make sure that your partner, Joanne attends our next meeting.

- We scheduled to meet again at your office next Thursday at 10:15.

Please let me know if there is anything here that needs clarifying, if I left something off, or if there is something else you want to make sure we address next Thursday

Best Regards,

[Your Name]

[Contact Info]

NOTES

- Generally I recommend SHORT emails. This email will be longer than any other I use. It's used very specifically after you have had a meeting (in person, by phone or by Skype) with someone and done a solid amount of discovery.

- Send this email (after modifying to fit the situation) after any meeting you have with a customer where you made progress towards a deal, but did not close it.

- The email should outline specifically their business pains THAT THEY EXPRESSED. Use their words, not yours. List their goals as they expressed. It's important that they pains and goals are what they said, not what you suggested.

- Make sure you also discuss the solution you are proposing *in general*. This is not a proposal so don't go too deep or list pricing.

- Document the next steps and action items you each agreed to at the end of the meeting. ** This is a key point. At the end of any meeting where the sale is still on the table, but has not closed make sure that you agree on action items for you and action items for them with deadlines for both. LOTS of deals stall out because of failure to do that one simple thing.

- Also at the end of that meeting, schedule your next meeting or discussion and document it.

- Ideally you should outline as many specific explicit benefits as possible. Be sure you are listing explicit benefits and not advantages. (Most people, even experienced sales pros, get this wrong. If you are not 100% sure you know the difference between explicit benefits and advantages please read this post (http://www.sb1.us/mistake)on my website.

- Specify their priority level for achieving the goal and their reasons why they said it isn't lower. This is a very powerful question to ask your leads. You can actually have them justifying to you within 4 questions you ask why they need to do this. To see exactly how to structure your discover conversations to do this and what questions to ask, get a copy of my Free Questions Report (instructions below)

- This email serves a few purposes. 1) it becomes great documentation and reminder for both of you what the meeting was about and what specifically was accomplished. If the deal stalls and revives at some point you'll both have details so you don't have to rehash as much, 2) it will separate you from every other person the meet with and make you appear more professional than everyone else, elevating the amount of trust they place in you. 3) it reminds them of the action steps they committed to, 4) it provides them with something concrete that they can show to others who may influence the deal... Giving you an opportunity to make sure that the highlights and important points are always kept front of mind, and 5) If you are dealing with a company with multiple decision makers and yours unexpectedly exits the company you'll have documentation to start with for the person who steps in behind them.

For a copy of The Questions Report : 45 of the Most Powerful Questions that convert prospects to customers faster than ever before, simply register this book by going to Bonus.The10SecondSale.com and enter your email and the code "questions" to get all the free resources from the book.

Or you can text "#questions" to to 1 (708) 221-9627 to have just the checklist emailed to you. We'll text you right back to ask for your email to send it to.

LOU Step 2

It's critically important to stand apart from the crowd with your customers and prospects. The Letter of Understanding will do that, but it's best to amp that up with an even more personalized touch.

One of the most effective ways to stand out and be remembered and thought of in a positive light is to send something in the physical mail. Everyone loves getting something nice in the mail. Cards are a great way to to that and it's super easy and a thank you card from you after your meeting will definitely be noticed.

Jacqueline Whitmore, a contributing author to Entrepreneur and etiquette expert not only recommends doing just that, but actually had sending a thank you note to someone at the county dump literally change her life. Twenty years ago she was on a recycling field trip with a group of people. After the tour she sent a thank you note to the tour guide who took them around and spoke with them. They had connected a bit on the tour, and he responded to the note by calling her up and asking her out on a date. After many more dates they got married. All because she took the time to send a thank you.

If sending a thank you note can land someone a spouse, imagine the power it can have on your business. I however, find the process of writing and addressing letters and cards to be a pain. I'm always looking for ways to make processes as easy as possible, and I've found one that works great for this.

One of the more effective tools I've used for years has been an online service that provides, addresses and sends the cards for me. These simple cards have helped me close hundreds of thousands of dollars in business over the past years. This service, SendOutCards offers full color greeting cards sent right from your computer keyboard — the system does all the work of printing, stuffing envelopes, adding a stamp, and mailing.

You choose from over 13,000 cards (or can design your own complete with photos) and can even have them scan your handwriting and signature to use in the cards. Everything is fully automated and you can even build touch campaigns to automatically send out other cards on a pre-set schedule. Additionally, there are gifts that you can choose from - motivational books, magazines, gift cards, or gourmet gifts of brownies, cookies, etc. to tag along with your card—all done online with a click of the mouse.

EMAIL COMMANDMENT # 8:
Add Physical Mail to Your Contact Campaign

To Try Sending a Card Online Yourself to a client (or someone you care about) for free simply go to http://www.sb1.us/20ecard

Your Most Productive Meeting Ever
Subject : Our meeting on Tuesday

Hi [lead's first name], I'm looking forward to our meeting Tuesday. As discussed I'll be at your office at 10:15. I've got your address as 123 Main Street, Suite 402, Chicago, 60601. If there are any changes please let me know. Otherwise, I'll see you on Tuesday.

On the agenda for the discussion is

1) your current lead conversion statistics and finding a plan to increase them to acceptable levels.

2) we'll take a look at your lead capture strategies to see where you can get more leads into your pipeline faster.

If there is anything else that you want to make sure we cover just let me know.

Also, here is a link to an article I wrote that may be of interest [link to something relevant]

All the best,

[Your Name]

[Contact Info]

NOTES

- It's rare for people to send meeting reminders these days so this will set you apart. It's even more rare for someone to send a proposed agenda. You'll be coming into the meeting appearing more professional from almost anyone else they've met with, before you even start.

- This can be used for either face to face, phone, or online meetings.

- Make sure that you are listing 1 or 2 agenda items that specifically relate to what you discussed when scheduling the meeting AND are high impact items for their business. That way when they are looking at their calendar to find room for something else that comes up at the last minute, your meeting isn't the thing that gets rescheduled. When they just have "Meeting with John" on their calendar it's easy for that to get pushed. On the other hand "Improve lead conversion and capture more leads" showing up on their calendar is less likely to seem low priority.

- Give them an opportunity to add something to the agenda. Often they will bring up something else you didn't already know to talk about, but is a hot button for them. Finding out ahead of the meeting gives you time to prepare in case it isn't a topic you would normally be ready to talk about on the fly.

Closing Templates

At some point, every sale is going to need to be closed. Ideally you'll do this in an actual conversation with the prospect either in person or on the phone. In some cases though you'll have to send an email that deals with an objection or stall. The templates that follow are some of my favorites to use when this happens. I've included these templates in the "closing" section since pitching, overcoming objections and closing are all parts of the same step of the sales cycle.

To learn more about my easy 4.5 step sales cycle that any coach, consultant or independent professional can use to close more business faster than ever before please take a look at my #1 Amazon Best Selling Book on Sales and Selling called Team of One: Get The Sales Results of a Full-Time Sales Team Without Actually Having One. You can check it out at http://www.teamofonebook.com

We are going with a competitor

Subject : Sales Coaching

[Prospect first name],

I got your message about deciding to sign up with another vendor for the training and coaching of your sales team. I appreciate the opportunity you've given me to show you how Sell Brilliantly can help you attain more sales.

I thought it would be helpful to quickly go over some ways we are different, since some other training options might seem similar on the surface.

Unlike other training companies, our training is not delivered by full time trainers. We use full time front line sales people who happen to be great trainers and do small amounts of training. This ensure you are learning

from someone who's skills are fresh and
work in the real-world today.

All the best,

[Your Name]

[Contact Info]

NOTES

- Like I said early about dealing with objections, an email or voicemail that your lead is going with a competitor is another case where email just does not create the impact you want. I can not stress enough how important it is that when you hear from a prospect that they are going with a competitor, what you need to do if you are going to have any chance to salvage the deal is SPEAK to them. What's the best way to get a chance to speak to a prospect? Pick up the phone and call them. If they don't pick up don't leave a message (this is one of the rare times I say don't leave a message. In most cases, if you bothered to pick up the phone, leave one). Wait a couple hours and try them again. Only then will you leave a voicemail and send an email.

- Point out 1 or 2 differences that you found out in discovery are important to them.

- Do not wait for a reply. Try calling them again either later that day, or the next day… Or both.

- Do not be tempted to do a brain dump in the email about all the reasons why they are making the wrong choice. Highlight 1 or 2 and ask for a conversation.

Reply to Being Turned Down

Subject : Sales Coaching

Hey [Prospect first name],

Thanks for taking the time to respond.

What could I have done to win your business?

I know you are busy but any guidance will vastly help me improve!

All the best,

[Your Name]

[Contact Info]

NOTES

- I can't stress enough how important it is when you get the "I'm going with a competitor email" that your first response is to pick up the phone an call them. Don't leave it to email to assume you hit the right hot buttons.

- I use this email only after using the prior email and getting no response.

- Acknowledge and appreciate them emailing you back.

- Asking for help understanding will often get a reply. You may not be able to do anything about it at this point, but the feedback can prove invaluable.

Lack of Urgency
Subject : Sales Appointments

Hey [Prospect first name],

Since our last conversation, I thought about something you said when we first talked. You mentioned that you currently meet with 3 new prospects each week in person and than you close one of those every other week. That means you are bringing in 24 new clients each year.

I heard from a client yesterday that just the work we did on scheduling appointments for him, netted him 1 extra appointment each week even though he was turning down 1 appointment each week he previously would have taken, since he now knew up front it wasn't a real lead. If we implemented just that one strategy for you, it would result in an extra $180k in additional revenue for you this year. That would more than cover hiring the production assistant you want so you can take a bit more time away from the office.

Let's schedule 30 minutes either to talk about the strategy and review if doing a smaller package just focused on that could work.

All the best,

[Your Name]

[Contact Info]

NOTES

- As I've said with other objections before, the first thing you'll want to do is call, not email. Email in this case is a last resort.

- When a prospect isn't progressing because they don't have urgency it's usually because they are not connecting the dots from what you do to the real end result that they want. Using their scenario and their numbers that they gave you and THEIR answer to what they ultimately wanted connect those dots for them as a reminder. If you haven't picked up a copy of The Questions Report yet to learn exactly how to do this, details on getting a copy follow.

- As usual, don't make this the end of your email chain. If you don't get a reply within 1 business day call them again.

For a copy of The Questions Report : 45 of the Most Powerful Questions that convert prospects to customers faster than ever before, simply register this book by going to Bonus.The10SecondSale.com and enter your email and the code "questions" to get all the free resources from the book.

Or you can text "#questions" to to 1 (708) 221-9627 to have just the checklist emailed to you. We'll text you right back to ask for your email to send it to.

You're Too Expensive
Subject : Book Publishing Package

Hey [Prospect first name],

I just got your email, and before you get completely overwhelmed and other projects, I want to ask you a couple of quick questions about your pricing comment.

1. Is the total package price too high, or are you more concerned with how the payments are structured?

2. Are their components of the proposal that did not resonate with you as much, or which you felt may not have been critical to implement?

Sometimes we may get carried away and build a package for you that encompasses everything we could do together. If we restructure this to just the most critical, highest impact components, we could lower our price while still having considerable impact on your business.

Are you prefer a call tomorrow at

10:15?

    All the best,

    [Your Name]

    [Contact Info]

NOTES

- I'm going to repeat this again. When you get this objection from a client, don't hurry and hit send. Pick up the phone first. Email is still a last resort.

- Pricing objections or if the object that they don't have the money even if they think the price is reasonable sometimes occur because of the way you have structured the deal. Ideally you'll have had those conversations before your proposal, but it still comes up on occasion. In those cases I always want to re-examine if either a payment plan or a smaller initial project will get the job done. Often they can't come up with the cash for the entire project, but if you break it down to the easiest, quickest to implement high impact part you can get a small deal done. Then while working for the client you continue to build trust and sell the rest of the deal... all while they are paying you to sell to them.

- As usual, don't make this the end of your email chain. If you don't get a reply within 1 business day call them again.

Need to Get Approval From Our CEO, Partner, Mommy, etc

Subject : Sales Coaching

[Prospect first name],

I work with many CEOs who delegate marketing initiatives to their teams and then approve the final plan, so this is pretty common.

Based on our discussions we have put together a marketing plan for you that will increase your lead flow resulting in:

- An additional 25 to 60 additional phone call discovery sessions booked each month

- 5-8 additional new clients generated each month. That should result in $420,000 of additional revenue from these new clients after 1 year.

The additional revenues will allow you to hire more staff to reduce the required hours to be worked.

The plan we built for you includes several methods of increasing lead-flow and getting more people on your list without increasing the # of speaking engagements and requiring less than 2 hours each month of video generation. Additionally we will build a robust lead communication plan for you.

Often the best way of making sure the CEO fully understands our plan and is able to request any appropriate modifications is to schedule a brief 15 minute call or meeting with him to review the details. I have time Tuesday at 10:15 or 2:45. Also Wednesday is open all afternoon. What would be a good time for him?

All the best,

[Your Name]

[Contact Info]

NOTES

- Ideally you should not get this response from a prospect because you would have found out early in the sales process. Should this come up your existing letters of understanding come back into play. You'll want to go back to your LOU (Letter(s) of Understanding) from earlier meetings. Pull out the key challenges you uncovered as reference.

- Keep the email brief, but cover the highest priority issues. Issues they expressed, not what you may have suggested. For the message to resonate it needs to be their priorities.

- Make sure that you offer a couple time windows to make it easy for them to respond with an appropriate time.

Get the Contract Back

Subject : Scheduling Logistics

[Prospect first name],

I hope things have settled down for you after your training event. I sent over the contract last week and want to make sure you received it. Did you get a chance to review it? Are there any questions that I can answer?

I'm finalizing my schedule for delivering on the final phases of another contract and want to make sure that we get your first sales process overhaul meeting scheduled. Does next Tuesday or the following Wednesday work for you?

All the best,

[Your Name]

[Contact Info]

NOTES

- Again keep it brief.

- Pick one of the first stages of your deliverables from the proposal and bring up scheduling for it. It raises urgency about getting access to your time and calendar.

- Make sure that you offer a couple time windows to make it easy for them to respond with an appropriate time.

Get the Contract Back 2

Subject : Getting your sales scripts started

Hey [Prospect first name],

I'm really looking forward to working together!

Attached is our agreement.

To keep things moving forward, can you get this back to me by Friday at 3pm. We'll be able to get your prospecting and discovery scripts done that way by the end of the month.

All the best,

[Your Name]

[Contact Info]

NOTES

- Before sending this email and if the deal size warrants it you can meet in person to get the document signed. If not, you'll definitely want to look at Docusign or Echoing so you have an electronic way to do it and are not waiting for physical mail.

- Again keep it brief.

- Pick one of the first stages of your deliverables from the proposal and bring up scheduling for it. It raises urgency about getting access to your time and calendar.

- Make sure that you offer a couple time windows to make it easy for them to respond with an appropriate time.

Welcome Email to New Signed Client
Subject : Welcome!

[Prospect first name],

I'm really looking forward to working together! My name is [name] and I'll be your account coordinator. My role is to ensure that you have everything you need so we together Sell Brilliantly and you can achieve your goals of:

- Building a full set of sales scripts for you

- Doubling the # of sales appointments your team sets weekly

- Increasing by 25% the amount of new leads hitting your funnel each week.

To get started, can you give me a couple of dates/times you are available next week so I can schedule David to complete phase 1 of the design process. He'll need 30 minutes with you to start out, and then 45 minutes with your top rep and 30 minutes with an average performer.

Once we have the session scheduled, I'll get you the initial script questionnaire that we'll need back at least 1 business day ahead of time.

Again, I'm looking forward to working with you! If you have any questions please don't hesitate to contact me directly.

All the best,

[Name]

[Contact Info]

NOTES

- When you bring a new client on board and have another team member who will be working closely with them, have that person send a quick short introductory email.

- If it's all you, just rework the email to take out the introduction, but still send your initial steps on how to get started even if you think they already know.

- Bonus idea, Use SendOutCards to send a Thank You card and Brownies! It's always a big hit.

Miscellaneous Templates

There are another of other reasons you'll want to email customers that don't directly relate to moving a particular opportunity forward, but still impact your sales. In this section you'll find some of my favorite templates to use when asking for advice, for references, referrals, or testimonials. You'll also find great ways to stay top of mind with your customers, to get introduced to specific people, and to double the chances that your voicemails will be returned.

Asking for Advice From a Stranger
Subject : Greetings from a fellow LifeBook member

[Prospect's first name]

I was doing some research for a

project on integrating sales teams after a merger and came across your profile on LinkedIn. I noticed that you too have attended LifeBook and that you've some great experience in that area. I'm on a mission to build some resources to help others go through the same thing and would love to ask you 3-5 quick questions about your experience with that.

Would you be available for a quick chat by phone or over coffee this Wednesday or Thursday at 10am? I'm also free anytime on Friday.

All the best,

[Your Name]

[Contact Info]

NOTES

- Mention a common connection in your subject line. It can be a mild connection, but do some research to find something. LinkedIn is a great place for this.

- Make the time commitment you are asking for seem minimal and low risk by specifying it's just 3-5 questions. Even if you ideally want more from them, you lower your chances by asking for a lot up front. Show them in the quick conversation that you are worth more of their time. Even if you don't get the full 2 hour interview you really want, a 10 minute 4 question interview to establish a personal connection can be tremendously valuable.

- Offer 2 specific times and one general time block to increase the chances of getting a time match, but not over complicating it.

Ask a Customer for a Referral
Subject :

[Customer's first name]

Great catching up with you today. I'm thrilled to hear how many more appointments you are running and deals you are closing since implementing the sales process and scripts we implemented for you.

Since we've been working together for almost a year now and I value your feedback, I would appreciate it if you would consider recommending me to a colleague or business contact that may have a gap in their own sales processes. Sell Brilliantly can help business of of any type find ways to close more deals faster. Please let me know your thoughts on who may be appreciative of the results I could bring them.

All the best,

[Your Name]

[Contact Info]

NOTES

- This works best when paired with a phone call first to ensure the client is happy and successful with the solution you've brought them.

- Be brief, but remind them of how you may be able to help others.

- If you get no reply, follow up with a phone call within a week.

- If the value you've brought to them is solid, it is not necessary to offer something in return for a referral. You can always add one in later, but you'll get more valuable feedback and likely a stronger referral if they are doing it just based on their relationship to you and truly believing their contact would benefit from what you do, rather than trying to think of someone so they can get your Xbox, Free Coffee, or whatever you are inclined to offer.

Ask a Customer to be a Reference

Subject : Help closing a new client.

[Customer's first name]

As a long time customer of ours I know you see the benefit to having a customized sales process and scripts for your business.

Since deploying the playbook we designed for you, I understand you have:

- Experienced a 200% increase in the number of sales appointments your team runs

- An increase in monthly revenue of $47,000

- Decreased time to train new sales reps

- And had your retention of sales reps double

I have a new client just about ready to come on board. It's a substantial client for me, but before signing the agreement he'd like to talk to an existing client for no more than 15 minutes. I value both your business and your time, so I wouldn't ask if I didn't know it would make a difference and that he is serious and close to becoming a client.

Obviously I'd like to make this happen as soon as possible. Would you have 15 minutes in the next few days that you could speak to him by phone? And 10 minutes for me so I can give you a snapshot of what they are looking for?

All the best,

[Your Name]

[Contact Info]

NOTES

- Never, Never, Never, give out a customers contact info to a prospective client blind. Check with your customer first. It's much more professional, and critical that you know that at this moment in time they are still inclined to say good things about you. Never assume that they will.

- Remind them of specific results, or specific things they have told you they have achieved as a result of working with you.

- Make sure that you ask for time to brief them personally before the call. This lets you a) gauge how enthusiastic they really will be on the phone, and b) ensure that you let them know about some of your prospects hot buttons.

Ask for a Testimonial

Subject : Can I quote you?

[Customer's first name]

As a long time customer of ours I know you see the benefit to having a customized sales process and scripts for your business.

Since deploying the playbook we designed for you, I understand you have:

- Experienced a 200% increase in the number of sales appointments your team runs

- An increase in monthly revenue of $47,000

- Decreased time to train new sales reps

- And had your retention of sales reps double

I am overhauling my website and looking for customers to highlight. I was wondering if you could give me a quote that I can use on my website. Ideally I'm looking for something link this :

"David completely changed the
direction of our business. I dread
meeting with prospective clients because
most of the time was wasted. David
turned that around. I now am able to
determine which are likely prospects and
which are not before the meeting, and
went from turning 1 out of 10 to 1 out
of 4 of those meetings into paying
clients." - Bob Barker, ABC Box Company

Is that cool?

All the best,

[Your Name]

[Contact Info]

NOTES

- You can tweak this email if you are looking for video or audio testimonials.

- Remind them of specific results, or specific things they have told you they have achieved as a result of working with you.

- When you are looking for a quote, I suggest you supply a sample of what you are looking for. If you are asking multiple people, supply them each with a different sample. Because you made it easy, you will get some enthusiastic people simply write back saying "Yes, what you wrote is perfect. You can use that."

Getting a Testimonial 2
THIS IS A 2 EMAIL SEQUENCE

Email 1 Subject: John, I need your help

[Customer Name],

Regular feedback is critical to me being able to continue to meet customers needs.

Was my Sell Brilliantly Sales Course interesting and useful for you? If yes, how has the course helped you? If not, why?

Any feedback you can provide will be extremely helpful.

All the best,

[Your Name]

NOTES:

- Step 1 is to get some basic feedback from them so you know for sure how they feel about your product, service or course. This simple email does that.

- When they reply and assuming their feedback is positive, then I craft a testimonial using their wording and include it in email 2.

- If you get unsolicited positive feedback you can craft a testimonial the same way and jump straight to email 2.

Email 2 Subject: re: John, I need your help

Hey [Customer Name],

I am thrilled to hear that you got so much value from my course!

If you have further questions about it don't hesitate to ask anytime.

I also have a question for you:

Could I get a short testimonial from you about my course? It'd be extremely helpful.

It could look something like this (I made it based on your feedback):

"The course is really well made. It was clear and understandable. I didn't even have to get all the way through it before I noticed my sales increasing. I learned A LOT from your section on questioning and started seeing an immediate difference in my sales meetings as a result. I recommend the course to anyone who's income is dependent on their ability for their prospects to naturally want to become customers. I've made several times more in increased income than the course cost in just the first 120 days."

Let me know if that looks good, or please adapt it to better fit your experience.

Thanks in advance!

All the best,

[Your Name]

[Contact Info]

NOTES

- Supplying the ideal testimonial from the words they used in their feedback makes it easy for them. They've essentially already said it, you just spruced up the wording.

- As long as they gave you good feedback, you'll get a large percent of those you send it to reply simply saying to go ahead and use what you suggested.

Asking Who to Talk to

Subject : XYZ Delivery

[Customer's first name]

It's been about a year now that you've had your custom sales scripts we developed for you deployed. Unless things have changed since our last talk I believe you have:

- Experienced a 200% increase in the number of sales appointments your team runs

- An increase in monthly revenue of $47,000

- Decreased time to train new sales reps

- And had your retention of sales reps double

Is that still accurate?

I was researching XYZ Delivery recently and I remembered that you had worked with them on several projects. I think they'd be a perfect prospect for my considering they are planning on expanding.

By any chance, do you know anyone over there who I should chat with? I'd love to learn more about their sales process to see if they'd appreciate the same kind of results you got.

Thanks for your help!

All the best,

[Your Name]

[Contact Info]

NOTES

- Again Be brief (notice that's a common theme), while reminding them of how you helped them.

- If you get no reply, follow up with a phone call within a week.

- When you've done a great job for clients, they often are very willing to put you in touch with others, but don't think about doing so and/or get stuck thinking about who to introduce you to. By asking them and making a suggestion of who, you've taken most of the mental work out of the equation for them.

- Even if your client can't introduce you to the final decision maker, getting a referral to an internal contact who can puts you in a much stronger position than if you were calling cold.

Birthdays, Anniversaries, etc.

Birthdays, Anniversaries, Children's Birthdays are not business check ins.

I know this is an email book, but I want to address Birthday messages. I get and see a lot of these. It's so easy for people to send a birthday email, or most a birthday message on Facebook. I'm going to recommend that you DO NOT do this though.

Everyone does this. Sending an email or a FaceBook post is very easy. It takes no time at all, usually very little thought, and usually the message you end up sending is bland and does nothing to make you stand out.

You want your contacts to take notice of you, sending a birthday or anniversary email or Facebook post just makes you blend in with everyone else.

Am I suggesting that you ignore birthdays? Absolutely not. I'm suggesting that you take the step of sending an actual card. Just like step 2 of the Letter of Understanding, a real physical birthday or anniversary card will be viewed differently than everyone else in their contact list.

There are a couple options for doing this.

1. You can do this the old fashioned way. There is likely a Hallmark store, a Walgreens, a CVS or a grocery store near you that carries cards. When you go in there for something else go to the card section and buy a bunch of cards so you have them on hand. You can likely buy stamps there as well. If you have a bunch on hand you can simply send them out about a week ahead of the birthday notices that come up in your calendar or on Facebook. (To see upcoming birthday's on Facebook click on "Events" and then next to "Birthdays this week" click "See All".

2. You can order cards online and have them sent for you. You can even have them delivered in your own handwriting if you want. There is a great online service that allows you to choose from Thousands of cards and send them out. It's actually cheaper than going to the store and much easier. If you want you

can even automate the process and have the system send all of your contacts a birthday card automatically. There are event gifts available to send with your card (the brownies are particularly good). As I mentioned for the LOU Step 2, the service I use for this is SendOutCards.

You can try it out yourself. I've made arrangements for you to be able to send one card to anyone you wish to test it. Simply go to http://www.sb1.us/20ecard

---

Ask for Introduction to a Specific Person

THIS IS A 2 EMAIL SEQUENCE

Email 1 Subject : Introduction to Peter Parker

Hey [Customer's first name]

I noticed on LinkedIn that you're connected to Peter Parker at the Daily Bugle. I would love to talk with him to get some advice about the Bugle.

If I promise to be respectful of his time, would you mind connecting me? I can send you a pre-formatted intro email to make it really easy for you.

Is that OK?

Thanks in advance,

[Your Name]

[Contact Info]

Email 2 Subject : Peter, meet David (helped my sales team tremendously). David, Meet Peter

[Your Customer's first name], here's a forward able email. It should be ready to send, but please feel free to edit as needed!

Thanks,

[Your Name]

———

Peter, David is an advisor of mine and helped me make huge gains in customer acquisition. He's excellent at helping companies improve sales results, without making customers feel like you are being pushy or salesy. He wondered if you could spare 10 minutes to chat on the phone.

David, can you take it from here?

Thanks,

David

NOTES

- This is a 2 step email.

- A direct intro to your prospect can often get you a connection much faster than other approaches, so when one of your contacts knows who you want to connect with, ask them.

- Be brief.

- Offering to send a pre-formatted email makes it super easy for them to say yes.

- If you get no reply, follow up with a phone call within a week.

- When you get a positive reply, you can use template 2 above ... Just tweak it to match the situation.

Stay Top of Mind

Subject : Interesting - Microsoft Exams must be getting easier!

Hey John,

Hope things are going well. It looks like it must be… I saw you guys made the Training Industry Top 20 list again.

I came across this article today about a 5 year old passing a Microsoft Certification exam and though you might find it interesting: www.articlelink.com

I'm writing a book on effectively using emails in one to one selling. I know a couple of your guys could use it from what we talked about recently. I'll send you a few copies once it's done.

All the best,

[Your Name]

[Contact Info]

NOTES

- One great way to stay top of mind with your prospects and customers and stand out from the crowd is to provide extra value to them whenever possible. Doing this can be particularly easy. When you come across an article, a book, or a infographic that you think is particularly interesting send it to the appropriate people. DO NOT just share it on your social media profile. You can do this sometimes as well, but I'm talking about when you see an article that you know would be of interest to particular people, send it directly to them. It shows you are thinking about them and their business and that you care. Here is an example that I actually just sent today.

- When I sent the email, I used the actual link to the article.

- I hadn't seen the Top 20 list I mentioned until I went to send the email. It took me 15 seconds to do a google search and come up with something to mention.

- Look for who else might be interested in the same article and replicate as possible to maximize the impact. In this case I looked at the rest of the Top 20 list and realized I had 32 other relevant connections in my address book that were in those other companies and might be interested in the article. I tweaked the last sentence about the book so it would be relevant to all of them and then had my VA send the same email individually to each of them. They'll all think I was targeting just them, but I got 33 touches out of what took me less than 4 minutes. That's only 7.2 seconds per email!

After a Voicemail

Subject : Sorry I missed you

Alternate Subject : Voicemail

Hey John,

Sorry I missed you on the phone today. I called because another client just started trying a new technique in their discovery meetings that doubled their discovery to proposal ratio. I remembered that was a metric you wanted to improve this year.

It's a pretty strategy to implement. I can walk you through it in no more than 10 minutes. Do you have time Thursday afternoon, or anytime on Friday?

All the best,

[Your Name]

[Contact Info]

NOTES

- This is pretty simple, you never know which your prospect will respond to better email or voicemail. Double your chances of getting a reply by doing both.

- Sometimes it's simply the seeing AND hearing your message that gets your prospect to respond. With this template it'll take less than 5 seconds to fire off the email.

Next Steps

You've made it to the end of my favorite email templates; templates which have helped me to close millions of dollars of sales myself.

You now have templates to tackle all kinds of sales situations. The most important part of this program, though, is the information which came before the templates. What you learned in that part of the book is how to craft your message and understanding the theory behind sending email to your prospects. Over time, as you email and test your results, you will find that you naturally build your own library of templates already customized for your business.

I've made all of the email templates in this book available for you to download as plan-text documents that you can load into any editor or email program that you'd like. To get those, simply register this book by going to Bonus.The10SecondSale.com and entering your email and the code "email" to get all the free resources from the book. Alternatively, you can text "templates" to book opt in phone # goes here to have the templates sent to you by telephone.

Appendix A -Email Commandments

There are some basic principles you want to follow when crafting your emails. You want your emails to get a response… Ideally start an actual conversation, and you should craft them accordingly.

EMAIL COMMANDMENTS:

1. Always have a call to action.

2. When possible make it possible for them to reply to their email simply by saying yes, or choosing from no more than 3 choices… 2 is better.

3. Make the paragraphs short and physically easy to read.

4. Make every sentence pass the "So What" test? If It

doesn't, kill it.

5. Make it SHORT. They should be able to read it in 10 seconds or less.

6. Email often. Most people under email, not over.

7. Always use THEIR Time Zone when referring to specific times.

8. Add physical mail to your sequence. Send a card or postcard. You will stand out.

For a downloadable and printable copy of these Email Commandments simply register this book at Bonus.The10SecondSale.com. Enter your email and the code "commandments" to get all the free resources from the book.

Or you can text "#commandments" to to 1 (708) 221-9627 to have just the checklist emailed to you. We'll text you right back to ask for your email to send it to.

Appendix B - Favorite Email Tools

Those that have worked with me have often asked my advice on how I get so much done. There really isn't much of a secret to it. I have spent a lot of time, energy, money building processes and rituals for myself to be as efficient as possible. I don't live by work smarter not harder. I focus on working smarter and harder.

The efficiency is not just a matter of rituals, but also of using the right tools. When it comes to emailing for sales these are some of my favorites!

Yesware is a very cool tool for sales and emails. It connects to your Gmail or Outlook and gives you tons of analytics about what happens after you click send. You'll know when your email was opened, forwarded, how many times it was opened and start seeing statistics about which emails you send get the most replies and opens. Knowing when an email is opened, allows you to target your next follow-up as precisely as possible. It'll allow you to send emails later, set reminders, and do mail merges for up to 200 people at once. If you run a sales team, it even will give you analytics across your entire team so you'll know which reps emails end up being the most responsive. I definitely recommend that you give it a try. The very helpful folks over there have fantastic support and have even allowed me to arrange a two-month free trial for you. Just head over to http://www.sb1.us/yesw

Text Expander saves me LOTS of time. It lets you type more with less effort! TextExpander saves your fingers and your keyboard, expanding custom shortcuts into frequently used text and pictures… This is my favorite time saving tool! It has literally saved me over 2.5 million key clicks in 2015. This Mac App is reasonably priced and you can get it at http://www.sb1.us/txte

Active Inbox turns Gmail into a task manager and keeps your Inbox clean. Never forget to follow up on another email. This is one of my 2 favorite tools. I'd probably give up my CRM before I gave up my ActiveInbox! Check it out at http://www.sb1.us/aihq

Unroll Me allows me to spend less time in my inbox dealing with newsletters, promotions from companies I want to stay to subscribed to an the like. It is a free app that consolidates your email subscriptions in one easy to use daily digest. Check them out at http://www.unroll.me

TimeTrade allows you to let your customers or prospects self schedule calls or meetings with you. It lets you configure when you want to be open to appointments and ties in to your calendar so it knows your availability. Then you can send a link and with a click of a few buttons your customer or prospect can see what meets their schedule and block off that time with you. It saves a lot of back and forth in scheduling. I do not recommend using this blind with new prospects, but when you have someone were scheduling has become challenging is very useful. I also use it in select mass emails. For example if I know that this week I'll be making 100 to 200 calls to existing prospects or customers about a select offer, I'll often send a teaser email to the whole list. In the email to let them know I'll be calling, and if they want to make sure we don't play phone tag they can schedule a time for my call and give them my TimeTrade link. This powerful technique allows the hottest leads from that list to call attention to themselves and ensures you'll actually connect with them rather than playing phone tag. It's a great way to maximize your time. They also have an incredibly reasonable fee structure. They definitely are under charge and for the value they provide. You can check them out at http://www.TimeTrade.com

Hemingway App is a free online tool that helps you make your writing bold and clear. Use it before you send emails to see how readable they are. It's great at catching when you've used Passive Voice. Visit them at http:/www.hemingwayapp.com

Your Email Signature can add dramatic credibility

to your emails. Your prospects and customers want to know why they should listen to you, why you are better than your competition and why they should feel you are credible. One of the fastest ways to do all of that is to leverage the automatic attachment that most people have when they learn that you are a best selling author. It's much easier than you may think. As a result of the specific training, templates and framework that I learned from my Mentor Mike Koenigs in his Publish and Profit Course I was able to get 2 complete books written, and launched to best selling status in less than 30 days each… All while working on them as side projects. For details about the self-paced training to do the same yourself visit http:// 0s4.com/r/HXVEZL. Or if you want Mike's team to help you put your book together they have an option for that as well. It's a little more expensive, but they make the process super easy and do most of the heavy lifting for you. Check out that option at http://0s4.com/r/KNI64E.

Automated **Real Physical Mail** through SendOutCards is an awesome way to send personalized cards, messages and gifts to your prospects and clients with the click of a few buttons. Setup automated campaigns, and send everything in your own handwriting. Nothing makes you stand out more from the crowd when you're the only one they got some thing real from. Send 1 card on me at http://www.sb1.us/20ecard.

44640094R00113

Made in the USA
Middletown, DE
12 June 2017